JOAN STEINER

LOOK-ALIKES Jr.

Photography by Thomas Lindley

Megan Tingley Books

LITTLE, BROWN AND COMPANY

New York ∾ An AOL Time Warner Company

For T.C.

The author wishes to express heartfelt thanks to Thomas Lindley for his superb photographic work, and to Megan Shaw Tingley, her editor, and Amy Berkower, her agent, for the unflagging support and enthusiasm they have shown for Look-Alikes from the very beginning. Thanks also go to Paul Richer of *Sesame Street* magazine, who originally commissioned several of these images.

Library of Congress Cataloging-in-Publication Data

Steiner, Joan (Joan Catherine)
    Look-alikes jr. / Joan Steiner ; photography by Thomas Lindley. — 1st ed.
      p.   cm.
    Summary: Simple verses challenge readers to identify the everyday objects used to construct eleven three-dimensional scenes, including a house, kitchen, bedroom, school bus, train, farm, and rocket.
    ISBN 0-316-71347-3
    1. Picture puzzles — Juvenile literature.   [1. Picture puzzles.] I. Title. II. Title: Look-alikes junior.
 I. Title.
   GV1507.P47S747   1999
   793.73 — dc21   99-11683

10 9 8 7

LB

Printed in the United States of America

The illustrations in this book are photographs of three-dimensional constructions created from found objects. The text was set in Formata. The display type is Albertus MT.

Come visit a land of wild surprises
Where common objects wear disguises!
Peanuts can look like a teddy bear,
Kiwi fruit like the pad for a chair.
At least fifty look-alikes in each scene
  (but two).
Find some or all—it's up to you.
The candy clock will count the hours,
As you test your detective powers...
And if you're really keeping track,
You'll find all listed at the back!

Happy Hunting!

To Look-Alike Land! We're blasting full throttle
On a spaceship that looks like a THERMOS BOTTLE.

Let's start our visit at this house.
That rock on the lawn looks like a TOY MOUSE!

Here's the kitchen, right down the hall.
That tea kettle looks like a red CHRISTMAS BALL.

The parlor's a cozy place to sit
In a chair that looks like an OVEN MITT.

Here's the bedroom and the bathroom as well.
The sink in the bathroom looks like a SHELL.

Here's the school bus, right on time.
Each rearview mirror looks like a DIME.

This classroom has books and paints and blocks.
The teacher's desk looks like a TISSUE BOX.

It's movie time—c'mon, boys and girls!
See those lights 'round the poster? They look just like PEARLS.

This construction site is right down the block.
The door of the cement truck looks like a LOCK.

I'd visit this farm if I had a chance.
The farmer's field looks like CORDUROY PANTS...

We hope that you will come back soon!
The signal post looks like a WOODEN SPOON.

It's signaling *"Bye, bye—for now!"*

EXTRA CHALLENGE

I don't always look the same
But I'm always long and lean.
Can you tell me: What's my name?
I'm found in every scene.

Hint: Keep a sharp lookout!

PLAY THE LOOK-ALIKES GAME

Search for look-alikes with a friend.
Take turns at finding *one.*
And when one of you is at wit's end,
That's when the game is done.

HOW TO COUNT THE LOOK-ALIKES

1. If more than one of the same object is used to make up *one* look-alike (such as ten pencils making up a fence), it counts as *one* look-alike. But if the same or a similar object appears elsewhere in the scene to make a *different* look-alike (such as a pencil appearing as a flagpole), it counts again.

2. Miniatures don't count as look-alikes unless they appear as something different from a larger version of themselves. For example, a toy car that represents a real car is not a look-alike. But a toy car that looks like a fire hydrant *does* count.

3. As long as you can identify an object, you don't have to get the name exactly right.

THE LOOK-ALIKES

*Asterisks indicate hard-to-find items —
for super sleuths only!*

ROCKET SHIP

- *53 Look-Alikes*

IN THE SKY: Rhinestones, star-shaped button, rhinestone ring, pearl, foil and plastic stars, yellow and orange M&M candies, marble, acorn, round button, silver snap, pearl earring, jingle bell, starfish, blue faceted bead, tiny seashell, Christmas ball ornament. ROCKET SHIP: **Left to right:** Wheat, batteries, spool of thread, birthday candle, Thermos bottle, rubber spatula, diaper pin, sticks of gum, sheet of loose-leaf paper, kernel of corn, red and green M&M candies, dime, spiral noodle, pencil-tip eraser, two-tone eraser, Lego piece, white pencil, marker pen, paintbrush, card of buttons, red paper clip, price tag, postage stamp, magnetic letter "T," nail clipper, metal buckle, shuttlecock. ASTRONAUT: Opera glasses, Ping-Pong ball, ponytail elastic, macaroni, striped seashell, screw, yellow button, tea bag, tubes of paint, clumps of cotton.

HOUSE

- *54 Look-Alikes*

TREES: **Left to right:** Rope, baguette, leather glove, dog figurine, green paper doilies, antler. GARAGE AND DRIVEWAY ITEMS: TV antenna, plastic hanger, paper matches, protractor, champagne cork muzzle, slate chalkboard. **Car:** Red shoe, peace symbol, buttons, barrette. **Lawn mower:** Sunglasses, padlock. LAWN, YARD, AND SIDEWALK: Towel, doggie treat, panpipe, chess piece (bishop), faucet aerator, pencil sharpener, wooden ballpoint pen, bunch of (artificial) grapes, embroidery hoop, catnip mouse, arrow, pencils, jigsaw puzzle pieces, poppy seeds*, mint candies (tricycle wheels). HOUSE: Indian corn, brick, matzoh, pretzel twists, tea bags, peanuts, dog biscuits, book, seashell, accordion expanding wall hooks, venetian mini-blind, comb, wooden forks, baby bottle nipple, birthday candles, gum erasers, coin purse, crayons, wallet, paper fastener, whistle.

KITCHEN

• *94 Look-Alikes*

ABOVE CUPBOARDS: Spools of thread, cherry tomato, postage stamp, small bar of soap, sea urchin shell, gold foil candy wrapper. CUPBOARDS, WINDOW, AND DOOR: Wallet, dollar bill, white dominoes, paint-chip strip, vacuum cleaner attachment, toggle buttons, crayon, cotton swabs, broccoli, cards of buttons, rulers, M&M candies (doorknobs). COUNTER AREA: **Left of stove:** Birthday candles, Chiclets gum, paper clip dispenser (with paper clips), tiny white buttons, nightlight, fuse, crayon tips, magnifying glass, three-outlet plug, envelope, powder puffs, bars of Ivory soap. **Stove:** Museum admission tag, tiny chess pieces, stick of gum (wrapped), tiny ravioli, harmonica, toy spiders, red Christmas ball ornament, Walkman, silver snaps, fever thermometers. **Right of stove:** Diaper pin, eye shadow applicator, spool of blue thread, acorn, cookie, door latch hook, sardine tin, bouillon cube, vegetable peeler, Gummy Bears candy, hair grip, pencil sharpener, bottle caps, sink plug, photographic slide, floppy disk, tiny black buttons*. STEP STOOL AND FLOOR: Staplers, dominoes, pages of calendar, white chocolate bar, pot-scrubber cloth. REFRIGERATOR AND CLOSET AREA: Mint candy, big white button, pencil-tip eraser, peanut, seven-day pill box, postage stamp, crochet hooks, eye shadow box, salt shaker, fake fingernail, small pencils, triple wall hook, toy teacups, individual coffee creamer, ice cube tray, dental mirror, paintbrush, green thimble, bubble gum (unwrapped), razor, tube of paint. TABLE AREA: Faucet aerator (ceiling light), Cheez Doodles, breadsticks, dog biscuits, embroidery hoop with fabric, silver thimble, jelly beans, Ritz cracker, paper fastener, wooden clothespins, place mat.

PARLOR

• *70 Look-Alikes*

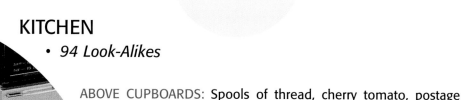

ALONG THE WALLS: **Left to right:** Maple seeds, seed packet, green ribbon, compact disc, brass drawer pull, kernels of corn, crayons, candy fruit slices, lasagna noodles, tiny white buttons, doorstops, tiny gold safety pins, leaves (real and artificial), gold buckle, gold bracelet, postage stamp. FURNITURE, LEFT-HAND SIDE: **Television:** Eye shadow box, ball-headed pin. **Cabinet:** Wrapped candy bar, Triscuit crackers. **Reading lamp:** Bell, ball-peen hammer, paperweight. **Wing chair:** Pea pod, candle, chess pieces (knights and bishops). **Dining area:** Christmas cookies, tambourine, spool of thread. **Rocker:** Barrettes, hairpins, slice of kiwi fruit. **Planter:** Napkin ring. FIREPLACE: Christmas ball ornament (well worn), mint candy, grommet*, toy diamond ring, marble, doll shoes, silk autumn leaf, magnets, cinnamon sticks, chocolate bar, paper binder clip. FURNITURE, RIGHT-HAND SIDE: **Grandfather clock:** Chess piece (pawn), toy compass, egg timer/hourglass. **Pink chair:** Two pincushions, doggie treat, pen nibs. **Sofa:** Toiletries/makeup bag, fruit-filled cookie, ravioli, angel-wing cookies. **Coffee table:** Roll of ribbon, bottle cap. **Easy chair:** Oven mitt. **Metal table:** Large compass, hose nozzle. **Side table:** Pencil, sea urchin shell, leather wallet insert, Pirouline tubular cookies, comb. ON THE FLOOR: Clothing label, place mat, spinach burrito wrapper, more postage stamps, Fig Newton cookie, slice of salami.

BEDROOM

- *67 Look-Alikes*

CEILING AND WALLS: Paper plate, (part of) bubble-blowing wand, sink plug, Ping-Pong ball, paper doll clothes, fruit cookies, tortilla chips, T-shirt, animal crackers, socks, cotton swabs, broccoli, pink barrette. BATHROOM: Postage stamps, dice, Wheat Thins crackers, paper umbrella, pacifier, seashell, tube of paint, jingle bells, tiny key. BEDROOM FURNISHINGS: **Bed:** Red crayons, peanuts (teddy bear), alphabet blocks, pasta spirals, bread roll, red comb. **Bookcase:** Pencils, sticks of gum, rubber ball, Lego pieces, Gummy Bears candy*. **Bureau:** Cap of toothpaste tube, spool of thread, green buttons, orange-and-white plastic harmonica, orange toothbrush. **Toy basket:** Ball of twine, plastic toothpick, toy flagpole stick, candle, red party streamer, chess piece (knight), crayon. **Laundry basket:** Calculator. **Desk and chair:** Pretzel twist, pretzel sticks, Ritz cracker, seashell, unshelled almond, dollar bill, yellow party streamer roll, sticks of green clay. ON THE FLOOR: Creme cookies, doll shoe, silver snaps, birthday candle, spiral seashell, gum eraser, cherry tomato, Life Saver candies, screw, dog biscuits, roll caps (for cap gun), tangerine, pot holder.

SCHOOL BUS

- *48 Look-Alikes*

ACROSS THE STREET: Pretzel sticks, spiral notepads, Life Saver candy, luggage tag, skirt fastener, Scrabble tiles, belt buckle, pink eraser, sponge penguin bath toy, pretzel twists, Triscuit crackers, cinnamon sticks, spool of thread, nuts (nuts-and-bolts type), tiny snap. BUS: Windshield ice scraper, hose sprinkler attachment, barrette, ruler, magnetic pick-up stick, birthday candles, tent stakes, pencils, tiny plastic clothespins, sports radio, pencil-tip eraser, buttons, felt-tip pen, M&M candies, chocolate-covered donuts, jacks, domino, crayons, diaper pins, thumbtack, nail clippers, dimes, pushpin, chess piece (bishop), wristwatch face. FOREGROUND: Broccoli, red pistachio nuts, green feathers, washcloths, popcorn, breadsticks, small slices of bread, pea pods.

CLASSROOM
• 67 Look-Alikes

CEILING: Loose-leaf binder with paper, marshmallows. ALONG WALLS: **Left-hand wall:** Spiral seashell, acorn cap, metal-edged ruler, dollar bill, balloons, blue comb, dog biscuits, starfish, lettuce, bull-dog paper clamp, paintbrush. **Back wall:** Yardstick, alphabet blocks, small box of tissues, red pencil sharpener, die, pencil-tip eraser, package-carrying handle, soap dish, raisin boxes, card of thumbtacks, paint box with brush, jelly bean, scallop seashell, wristwatch face, caramels, toy train freight cars, pencils (two kinds for easel), wishbone, playing card, two green books (chalkboard), sink plug, bird's egg, clear plastic coin purse, Goldfish crackers, brown rice*, paddleball toy, sticks of blue clay, feathers, spool of crochet thread. **Right-hand wall:** Paintbrush (flagpole), lollipop, button. IN CENTER OF ROOM: Spiral notepads, crayons, cut-off pencils, saltine crackers, price tag, slate chalkboard, wooden clothespins, white beads (square and round), wooden match, postage stamps (drawings), hook (hook-and-eye type), pineapple slice, white jar lid*, sticks of chalk, birthday candle, silver thimble, afro comb, large box of tissues, chess pieces (pawns), scissors, another postage stamp (book), serpentine party streamer.

MOVIE THEATER LOBBY
• 54 Look-Alikes

CEILING: Hubcap, jingle bell, gold buttons, jacks. HANGING LAMPS: Glass doorknob, wooden ballpoint pen with cap, doorbell, candle. LOBBY WALLS, ENTRANCEWAY, AND TICKET WINDOW: Red golf tees, red pick-up sticks, red pencils, bulldog paper clamps, string of pearls, red comb, playing cards, shelf brackets, coins (dimes and 100-peso pieces), silver ballpoint pens, nut picks, wrench, table knives, toy compass, toothbrush and cup holder, movie tickets. LOBBY FLOOR AND FREE-STANDING ITEMS: Pennies, gold hoop earring, meat thermometer, wooden ruler, jigsaw puzzle pieces, doorstops, paper clip dispenser (with paper clip), brass hose nozzle, tiny safety pin, protractor. REFRESHMENT STAND AREA: Paper fan, toothbrushes, plastic coin purse, pencil sharpener with shavings holder, alphabet noodles*, starfish, silver pencil sharpener, plastic thimble, cut-off crayons, digital watch, Lucite salt shaker/pepper mill, bouillon cubes, dice, address book with pencil, dollar bill, price tag, tiny watercolor paint box, harmonica, leather wallet, dental floss dispenser.

CONSTRUCTION SITE

- *94 Look-Alikes*

BEYOND THE FENCE: **Left to right:** Bricks, ink bottle, shoe polish tin, merchandise stamps, dog biscuits, broccoli, lipstick, Bingo cards, admission tickets*, address book, ice-cream cone, cookie wafers, dice, lantern, silverware storage tray, sardine tin, ball-point pen and holder, restaurant order pad. AIRPLANE: Tube of paint, guitar pick, tiny nut (nuts-and-bolts type)*, transparent button*. FENCE: Pretzel sticks. IN THE PIT: **Construction shack:** Spiral notepad, UPC label. **Yellow crane:** Walkman-style radio, staple remover, pencil, disposable-blade knives, hexagonal breakfast cereal, black buttons, squishy fishing lure. **Blue steamroller:** Candles, nail clipper, screw, magnetic letters and numbers (F, Z, 1, 7). **Black building frame:** CD storage rack, CD jewel cases. **Red excavator:** Camera, penknife, key holder, wind-up mechanical teeth, pushpin, gold bracelet, red foil stars. **Small yellow crane:** Toy giraffe, wooden matches. **Blue tower crane:** T-square/metal ruler, clear plastic ruler, box of matches, diaper pin, weighted fishhook. **White building frame:** Carpenter's folding rules (opened), wire shower caddies, matzoh, small bar of soap*, sticks of gum. **Orange trailer:** Carpenter's level, orange Life Saver candies. **Cement mixer:** Mustard bottle, postage stamp, padlock, (part of a) flexible drinking straw, metal whistle with orange cord, small pencil, plastic whistle, staplers, shoehorn, birthday candle, rolls of black electrician's tape, jacks, spool of green thread. **Individual items at the site, left to right:** Desk lamp, brownies with nuts, carpenter's folding rule (folded), shelled walnuts, coffee beans, gum erasers, ballpoint pen, cotton swabs, felt-tip pen, embroidery hoop. FORE-GROUND: Birdseed, crayons, dog biscuits, small slices of bread, tweezers, big black button, (Note: tiny bucket is a miniature rather than a look-alike), cinnamon sticks, peppermint stick, red M&M candy, clamps, breadsticks, blue jeans label.

FARM SCENE

- *70 Look-Alikes*

TO LEFT OF ROAD: **From top:** Plaid zippered bag*, throw pillows, green pot scrubber, green gumdrops, leaf-shaped mint candies, sock, washcloth, metal hinge, (Note: toy truck is a miniature rather than a look-alike), dime wrapper with dime, lipstick, bunch of (artificial) grapes, doormat, peanut (in wagon)*, wagon-wheel pasta, Tater Tots, (part of) stuffed animal, potatoes (red and white), parsley (in many places), pot holder, angel-wing cookie, green beans (several places), peacock feathers, corduroy pants, red hair grip, mailing tape dispenser, black snap (steering wheel)*, inflation needle, paper clip, big button, assorted nuts (hazelnuts and Brazil nuts), burnt matchsticks, green jelly beans (in several places), green hair ties ("scrunchies"). ROAD: Tan necktie, hamster food. TO RIGHT OF ROAD: Gold pot-scrubber cloth, pastry cutter, green dog biscuits, pot holder loom with green loops, dark green velvety glove, toy fawn, batteries (AA and AAA), checkered place mat. BARN: Toolbox, earring, green padlock, cake decorator tip, thimble, ladle, plastic drinking straw, key, aerosol can, toy train track, dominoes, candy fruit slice, cotton swabs, croutons. BARNYARD: Cinnamon sticks, fur (two kinds), brown crayon, old-fashioned roller skate, pencils (two kinds), ball of twine, coffee can, copper funnel, garlic cloves, jigsaw puzzle piece, peanut, Brazil nut, coffee beans.

CHOO-CHOO TRAIN

- *46 Look-Alikes*

SMOKE: Clumps of cotton. TRAIN: **Locomotive:** Sink aerator, jar of model paint, tiny brass bracket, roll of film, lamp socket, yellow Life Saver candy*, flashlight, spiral notepad, toy school bus, pennies, spool of black thread, big black buttons, tiny paper binder clip, can opener, wrench, (artificial) daisies. **Tender:** Tea tin with tea, sewing machine bobbins (on next two cars as well). **Passenger car:** Watercolor paint box, pencils, birthday candles, melba toast, afro comb, package-carrying handle, dog biscuits, dollar bill, corncob holder. **Freight car:** Ruler, batteries, fishing float, tiny key, more pennies, wallet, dollar bills, clothing label. LANDSCAPE: Green blanket, tweed jacket, woolen hat, parsley, jigsaw pieces. SIGNAL POST: Wooden spoon, top of a Thermos, red and green Life Saver candies. TRACKS: Brown lamp cord, sticks of gum (unwrapped).

ANSWER TO EXTRA CHALLENGE: Pencil.

JOAN STEINER

is a graduate of Barnard College and a self-taught artist. Her Look-Alikes books have sold more than one million copies and have been published in sixteen countries around the world. The recipient of numerous art and design awards, including a Society of Illustrators Award and a National Endowment for the Arts fellowship, Ms. Steiner lives in Claverack, New York.

Accolades for *Look-Alikes® Jr.*

★ "In Steiner's hands, the ordinary becomes extraordinary."
—*Publishers Weekly* (starred review)

◆ "Dazzling ingenuity . . . amazing." —*Kirkus* (pointer review)